BRANDY S. FLORY

HOW TO LIVE YOUNGER AND LONGER

16 ways to live younger and longer supported by science

Contents

TRY NOT TO EAT TOO MUCH

Association between calorie confirmation and life expectancy right presently creates a lot of interest. Animal examinations suggest that a 10-half decline in normal calorie confirmation could augment the most outrageous future. Examinations of human masses lofty for life range moreover notice joins between low-calorie utilization, a long future, and a lower likelihood of disease. Calorie limits could help with diminishing excess body weight and gut fat, the two of which are connected with more restricted futures

That is said, too much calorie admission is often illogical and can integrate negative optional impacts, such as extended hunger, low inner intensity level, and a decreased sex drive.

EAT A PLANT-BASED DIET

A plant-based diet stresses food sources like fruits, vegetables, and beans, and cutoff points are food sources like meats, dairy, and eggs. From that point, more limitations could be placed and set up according to how strict you want to be. It might totally kill food sources from animals or simply limit admission. That implies meat and fish is not totally forbidden rather you can eliminate how often you eat those them.

To live more youthful and longer, your eating routine ought to be generally normal plant-based, unite beans and a dab of a piece of meat. Eating up a wide variety of plant food assortments, similar to normal items, vegetables, nuts, seeds, whole grains, and beans, may lessen disease endanger and propel life range.

For example, numerous examinations interface a plant-rich eating routine to a lower opportunity of unexpected death as well as a reduced bet of harmful development, metabolic condition, coronary disease, wretchedness, and frontal cortex debilitating. These effects are credited to laying out food sources' enhancements and disease avoidance specialists, which integrate polyphenols, carotenoids, folate, and L-ascorbic corrosive.

Likewise, a couple of assessments interface veggie darling

and vegan eats less, which are regularly higher in plant food assortments, to a 12-15% lower chance of startling death. Comparable examinations moreover report a 29-52% lower risk of passing on from harmful development or heart, kidney, or compound-related disease. Some investigation suggests that the bet of startling death and certain diseases increases with more noticeable meat use.

Regardless, various examinations report either nonexistent or much weaker associations — with the unfriendly results seeming, by all accounts, to be expressly associated with taking care of meat Vegetarians and veggie darlings similarly overall will commonly be more prosperous aware than meat eaters, which could generally figure out these revelations. In the United States, having a low-quality eating routine is the greatest indicator of early demise. An exemplary American eating routine that is high in soaked and trans fats, sodium, and handled meat puts you in a difficult spot with regards to wellbeing and life span, while an eating routine that advances entire food sources and plant-based fixings seems to make the contrary difference.

For sure, the vast majority who embrace this approach to eating do it for the potential medical advantages. There have been numerous heart benefits connected to eating along these lines, such as decreased cholesterol. A few examinations propose that eating a plant-based diet might further develop ripeness boundaries, and it likewise may lessen your gamble of creating [type 2] diabetes. A very much arranged plant-based diet can be ok for everybody, including infants, kids, and individuals who are pregnant or nursing.

As the accompanying examination proposes, a plant-based diet might assist with lessening the probability that you'll require drugs, bring down your gamble of weight and hypertension, and perhaps help forestall or oversee type 2 diabetes and coronary illness. Here is a more critical gander at conceivable plant-based diet benefits.

a. A Reduced Risk for Type 2 Diabetes

In a survey distributed in July 2018 in JAMA Internal Medicine, scientists found that following a plant-based diet (one that included food sources like natural products, veggies, vegetables, nuts, and entire grains) was related to a lower chance of type 2 diabetes. The nine examinations required around 307,100 members, and were adapted to elements, for example, smoking status and exercise recurrence that in any case might have impacted the outcomes. Analysts hence found that the lower risk was because of members' eating regimen decisions.

The justification for this lower chance of type 2 diabetes might be the further developed capability of beta cells, which assist with creating insulin (the chemical that keeps glucose levels stable). The past examination has noticed that as type 2 diabetes advances, beta cell capability declines and this can cause risky changes in glucose levels. Yet, a randomized preliminary found that after only 16 weeks following a plant-based diet, members would do well in beta cell capability and insulin responsiveness contrasted and the benchmark group — also further developed weight files (BMIs) and less gut fat.

b. A Healthier Weight and Blood Sugar Level in People With Diabetes

In another review, which was distributed in September 2019 in Translational Psychology, analysts presumed that this diet is useful for helping digestion, overseeing weight, and lessening irritation, particularly among individuals with stoutness and those with type 1 and type 2 diabetes. One survey proposed that a plant-based diet decidedly affects profound and actual prosperity, personal satisfaction, and general wellbeing for individuals living with type 2 diabetes, while likewise working on actual markers of the condition in this populace.

c. A Reduced Risk of Heart Disease

One review connected eating less wealthy in sound plant food sources (like nuts, entire grains, natural products, veggies, and oils) with an essentially lower chance of coronary illness.

Following an eating routine wealthy in plant food sources and lower in creature food sources are related to a 16 percent lower chance of cardiovascular illness and a 31 to 32 percent lower hazard of death from cardiovascular sickness. There are a few elements in play here, including the way that plant-based diets can diminish cholesterol levels and lower irritation, as per a case report.

d. A Reduced Risk of Cancer

Research from the United Kingdom took a gander at around 475,000 grown-ups who were sans disease at the gauge. The members were sorted as normal meat eaters, low meat eaters, fish eaters, and vegans and followed up to check their rate of disease 11.4 years after the fact. The low meat eaters, fish eaters, and vegans had a lower chance of colorectal, bosom, and prostate tumors when contrasted and normal meat eaters. The scientists suspect a low BMI could likewise be a contributing element to the lower disease risk. One more review zeroed in on bosom disease explicitly and found that people who most firmly followed a plant-based diet had a 67% lower chance of bosom malignant growth than the people who followed it the least.

e. A Healthier Brain

A plant-based diet could be useful for both your body and your brain. While research is blended, one review including more than 3,000 grown-ups saw as staying with a plant-based diet was connected with better mental capability, including long haul memory and chief capability.

f. A Longer Life

Some exploration connects an eating routine containing more elevated levels of plant protein with a slower pace of early demise from all causes; one survey of studies (including more than 715,000 members) found that members whose diets contained the most plant-based protein had a 6 percent lower chance of sudden passing than people who consumed less protein generally. One investigation of 135,000 people tracked down a connection between expanded admission of organic products, vegetables, and vegetables and a lower hazard of all-cause early demise, with members receiving the greatest wellbeing rewards at three to four servings each day — a sum that anybody following a plant-based diet is probably going to meet.

Nonetheless, absolutely staying with plant-based food sources probably won't slice it you'll have to focus on the nature of the food sources you're eating, since there are a lot of undesirable food sources that qualify as plant-based, for example, potato chips and french fries. Unfortunate plant-based food sources will build your gamble of weight gain and ailments like coronary illness.

Something else you ought to know about: When you first change to a plant-based diet, you might see an increase in defecations, the runs, or stoppage. That is because many plant-based food sources are stacked with fiber, and fiber standardizes defecations. Consider slowly consolidating plant-based food sources in your eating regimen to give your body time to change, and make certain to drink a lot of liquids while you're doing the change to eating more plants and subsequently.

Generally, eating a plant-based diet will look at the cases of the multitude of significant supplements. A very much arranged plant-based diet can be healthfully sufficient and especially plentiful in fiber, vitamin A, L-ascorbic acid, and potassium due to every one of the products of the of the soil that is commonly eaten.

However, assuming you choose to take the plant-based diet to a higher level and avoid all types of meat, you might have to watch out for your degrees of vitamin B12 and choline. "Vitamin B12 is tracked down basically in meat sources, and the two best wellsprings of choline are egg yolks and liver.

A Food List of What to Eat, Limit, and Avoid on a Plant-Based Diet

What to Eat and Drink

Vegetables (counting kale, spinach, Swiss chard, collard greens, yams, asparagus, chime peppers, and broccoli)

Fruits (like avocado, strawberries, blueberries, watermelon, apples, grapes, bananas, grapefruit, and oranges)

Entire grains, (for example, quinoa, farro, earthy colored rice, entire wheat bread, and entire wheat pasta)

Nuts (pecans, almonds, macadamia nuts, and cashews all count)

Edible seeds (like flaxseed, chia seeds, and hemp seeds)

Beans

Lentils

Espresso

Tea (counting green, lavender, chamomile, or ginger)

What to Limit (or Avoid Entirely, Depending on the Plan You Choose)

Dairy (counting milk and cheddar)

Meat and poultry (like chicken, hamburger, and pork)

Handled creature meats, like wieners and franks

Every creature item (counting eggs, dairy, and meat on the off chance that you're following a veggie lover diet)

Refined grains, (for example, "white" food varieties, similar to white pasta, rice, and bread)

Desserts (like treats, brownies, and cake)

Improved refreshments, like pop, and natural product juice

Potatoes and french fries

Honey (if vegetarian)

What to Limit (or Avoid Entirely, Depending on the Plan You Choose)

Dairy (counting milk and cheddar)

Meat and poultry (like chicken, hamburger, and pork)

Processed meats, like wieners and sausages

Every animal protein(counting eggs, dairy, and meat on the off chance that you're following a vegetarian diet)

Refined grains, (for example, "white" food varieties, similar to white pasta, rice, and bread)

Desserts (like treats, brownies, and cake)

Improved drinks, like pop, and organic product juice

Potatoes and french fries

Honey (if vegetarian)

EAT A LOT OF NUTS

Nuts are a healthy awe-inspiring phenomenon. They're affluent in protein, fiber, cell fortifications, and accommodating plant compounds. Besides, they're a fantastic wellspring of a couple of supplements and minerals, similar to copper, magnesium, potassium, folate, niacin, and supplements B6 and E. A couple of examinations show that nuts significantly influence coronary sickness, hypertension, disturbance, diabetes, metabolic condition, gut fat levels, and, shockingly, a couple of sorts of infections. One examination found that people who consumed something like 3 servings of nuts every week had a 39% lower peril of unexpected passing.

In like manner, two continuous overviews including more than 350,000 people saw that individuals who ate nuts had a 4-27% lower chance of kicking the pail during the survey period — with the best reductions found in the people who ate 1 serving of nuts every day.

MODERATE YOUR ALCOHOL UTILIZATION

Significant alcohol use is associated with liver, heart, and pancreatic contamination, as well as an overall extended possibility of early end. Moderate usage is connected with a reduced likelihood of a couple of sicknesses, as well as a 17–18% decrease in your bet of startling passing. Wine is considered particularly valuable due to its high blissful of polyphenol cell fortifications. Results from a 29-year study showed that men who leaned toward wine were 34% less leaned to sit back than individuals who were inclined toward brew or spirits.

Additionally, one review saw wine to be especially cautious against coronary ailment, diabetes, neurological issues, and metabolic condition. To keep used moderate, it is recommended that women go all in units or less every day and a constraint of 7 consistently. Men should keep their regular admission to under 3 units, with a restriction of 14 consistently.

Thu sly, there is a convincing explanation need to start savoring the occasion so that you don't, when in doubt, finish alcohol.

COMPANIONS AND COMMUNITY

Incorporate yourself with positive individuals who support you. Find a severe assistance to which you can relate. Going to such associations on different occasions consistently can add 4-14 years to your life. Put resources into your loved ones and family. Support your family with your time and love. Solid family bonds can add apparently perpetually to your life.

THINK ABOUT SUPPLEMENTS

Whether you eat well you're obviously lacking supplements colossal for sound creating. Here are some examples of supplements to support your diet for longevity.

Curcumin — the vitally dynamic compound in turmeric — has been displayed to have strong cell defensive properties, which are credited to its powerful cancer prevention agent impacts. A cycle called cell senescence happens when cells are quite isolating. As you age, senescent cells aggregate, which is accepted to speed up maturing and sickness movement. Research shows that curcumin enacts specific proteins that assist with postponing cell senescence and advancing life span. In addition, creature studies exhibit that curcumin battles cell harm and altogether increments life range. This compound has been displayed to delay age-related sickness and lighten age-related side effects also.

For these 5reason, turmeric admission is related to a decreased gamble old enough related to mental deterioration in people. You can expand your curcumin consumption by involving new or dried turmeric in the kitchen or taking turmeric or curcumin supplements.

L-ascorbic acid

L-ascorbic acid capabilities as a strong cancer prevention agent in your body, assisting with safeguarding cells from oxidative harm. It additionally assumes significant parts in safe capability, irritation guidelines, and numerous different cycles that are vital for sound maturing. Therefore you ought to keep an ideal admission of this nutrient to help wellbeing and safeguard against age-related conditions.

For instance, in a concentrate in 80 grown-ups with a typical age of 60, those with higher blood levels of L-ascorbic acid performed better on undertakings including consideration, center, memory, direction, review, and acknowledgment. L-ascorbic acid is additionally fundamental for skin wellbeing. Enhancing may further develop skin hydration, animate collagen creation, and defend against wrinkle advancement and untimely maturing because of sun openness.

Additionally, some proof recommends that enhancing with L-ascorbic acid works on safe capability in more established grown-ups. As more seasoned grown-ups have a higher gamble of sub-standard or lacking L-ascorbic acid levels than moderately aged or more youthful grown-ups, they might need to think about taking enhancements — particularly if their eating regimen is low in L-ascorbic acid rich food sources like products of the soil.

As well as following a solid eating routine and way of life, taking specific enhancements might assist with easing back the maturing system and advance a long, sound life

Collagen

As you age, the creation of collagen, a protein that keeps up with skin structure eases back, prompting sped-up indications of maturing like kinks. Some exploration proposes that enhancing with collagen might diminish indications of maturing, including kinks and dry skin. For instance, a 12-week concentrate on in 72 ladies showed that taking an enhancement that contained 2.5 grams of collagen — alongside a few different fixings, including biotin — each day essentially further developed skin hydration, harshness, and flexibility.

Other human investigations show that collagen enhancements might further develop skin versatility, decrease wrinkles, increment skin hydration, and further develop nail development. However these outcomes are promising, a large number of these investigations are financed by organizations that make collagen items, which might impact concentrate on results. Many kinds of collagen supplements are accessible, including powders and cases.

Crocin

Crocin is a yellow carotenoid color found in saffron, a well-known, expensive zest that is ordinarily utilized in Indian and Spanish food. Human and creature studies have shown that crocin offers numerous medical advantages, including anti-cancer, calming, against nervousness, upper, and antidiabetes impacts. It likewise safeguards against age-related mental degradation. Test-cylinder and rat review exhibit that crocin forestalls age-related nerve harm by restraining the creation of cutting-edge glycation finished results (AGEs) and responsive oxygen species (ROS), which are intensifies that add to the maturing system.

Crocin has likewise been displayed to assist with forestalling maturing in human skin cells by decreasing irritation and safeguarding against cell harm actuated by UV light. Since saffron is the world's most costly zest, it could be savvier to take a concentrated saffron supplement.

CoQ10

Coenzyme Q10 (CoQ10) is a cell reinforcement that your body produces. It assumes a fundamental part in energy creation and safeguards against cell harm. The research proposes that degrees of CoQ10 decline as you age. Enhancing by working on specific parts of wellbeing in more established individuals has been shown. For example, a 4-year concentrate on in 443 more established grown-ups exhibited that enhancing with CoQ10 and selenium worked on generally speaking personal satisfaction, decreased clinic visits, and eased back physical and mental crumbling. CoQ10 enhancements might work by lessening oxidative pressure, a condition portrayed by a gathering of free revolutionaries that speeds up the maturing system and the beginning of old enough related infection.

Also, CoQ10 enhancements might help heart wellbeing by decreasing firmness in your courses, bringing down pulse, and forestalling the development of oxidized cholesterol in your conduits.

MINGLE

I t's presumably a given that destruction unfavorably impacts your significant well-being, yet did you comprehend it can really influence your qualities and perhaps contract your life? The research proposes being desolate can ominously impact telomeres, the sections of DNA near the fulfillment of our chromosomes that gather each time a cell limits and may show how long we'll live. Longer telomeres are associated with every one of the more lazy growing, less age-related defilements, and by and large around additional perceptible fates. In an assessment of African dull parrots in enslavement, people who were housed alone had more limited telomeres and stood apart from individuals who stayed with a friendly bird. This finding keeps a making get-together of confirmation appearance that social segregation and different stressors can impede

CARE FOR YOUR SKIN

Science shows the state of your skin immensely impacts how elderly individuals think you are. To screen pleats and sun spots, wear sunscreen, and utilize care for Your Skin

Science shows the state of your skin gigantically impacts how elderly folks individuals think you are. To screen pleats and sun spots, wear sunscreen, utilize a crucial cream, and hydrate. You can too utilize a few normal fixings tracked down in the kitchen to make some anti_aging cream recipe. Models,

make your skin ruddy with rose water

What home cure fixings are generally suggested? Skincare specialists go wild about a blend of rose water, rice powder, and milk. Blend these three super fixings into a thick glue, then, at that point, apply the veil to your face and leave it on for 20 minutes. Rose water lights up your skin's appearance, rice assists your skin with creating more collagen to further develop versatility, and relieving milk eases up dim regions of the skin. In addition, this skincare home cure feels rich and scents awesome.

Light up your tone with lemon. Don't let dim spots and maturing skin sharpen your look. Utilize the astringent properties of lemon to ease up skin and age spots. Lemon levels out your complexion and lights up your appearance. There's no unique recipe, just put a little lemon juice on a cotton ball and apply it to your skin every day as a fortifying toner. You can likewise fit lemon into warm or cold water in the first part of the day to stimulate your whole body.

PONDER

As for keeping you lively, thought has been displayed to change the mind trulNeuroscientist at Harvard Medical School and Massachusetts General Hospital, drove evaluations including cerebrum consequences of meditators. It was discovered that individuals who had been reflecting for quite a while had expanded faint matter in the hear-skilled and material cortex, which are credits to the careful idea paid to breathe, sounds, and different overhauls during the assessment. She additionally found more dull matter in the cerebrum, the piece of the mind related to memory and course.

Meditators in their fifties had the real extent of weak matter in one piece of the prefrontal cortex as individuals in their twenties overlooking how the cortex is implied agreement as we age. Why not integrate this mind-supporting practice into your life? You could indeed figure out a good method for reflecting by utilizing a remote application.

EXERCISE

remaining really powerful can keep major areas of strength for you. As relatively few as 15 minutes of movement every day could help you with achieving benefits, which could consolidate an additional 3 extensive stretches of life. Also, your bet of startling passing could reduce by 4% for an additional 15 minutes of ordinary dynamic work. Another study saw a 22% lower opportunity to early pass in individuals who rehearsed regardless of the way that they worked out not the very proposed 150 minutes out of every week. People who hit the 150-minute proposition were 28% more unwilling to kick the pail early. Moreover, that number was 35% for individuals who rehearsed past this heading.

Finally, an investigation joins exciting development to a 5% more noticeable diminishing in risk diverged from low-or moderate-power practices thought about safe.

DO WHATEVER IT TAKES NOT TO SMOKE

Smoking is solidly associated with ailment and early downfall. By and large, those who smoke could lose up to 10 years of life and be on numerous occasions bound to pass on imprudently than individuals who never get a cigarette. Recollect that it's never past an opportunity to stop. One audit reports that individuals who quit smoking by age 35 may draw out their lives by up to 8.5 years.

Also, halting smoking in your 60s could add up to 3.7 years to your life. Halting in your 80s could regardless give benefits, actually.

HUMIDIFY YOUR HOME

Keep your skin delicate and energetic by adding a humidifier to your home. Ensure you place one in your room, so you can get no less than eight hours of added dampness. You may likewise need to add a humidifier to different rooms where you invest a ton of energy, similar to your lair or workspace. They're perfect for winter when the outside air is additional dry and humidifiers likewise help in summer since cooling eliminates moistness from the air.

PRIORITIZE YOUR JOY

eeling delighted can essentially construct your longevity. In reality, more cheerful individuals had a 3.7% lessening in early passing more than a 5-year focus on period An examination of 180 Catholic nuns inspected their self-uncovered levels of fulfillment when they initially entered the strict local area and later stood out these levels from their life expectancy. Individuals who felt generally happy at 22 years of age were 2.5 times bound to anyway be alive sixty years sometime later.

Finally, a study of 35 assessments showed that merry people could fulfill 18% longer than their less delighted accomplices

AVOID STEADY STRAIN AND STRESS

Strain and stress may in a general sense lessen your lifespan. For the event, women encountering tension or disquiet are purportedly dependent upon two times bound to elapse on from coronary sickness, stroke, or cell breakdown in the lungs. Basically, the bet of unexpected passing relies upon numerous times higher for fretful or centered men diverged from their more relaxed counterparts. If you're feeling stressed, chuckling and good reasoning could be two basic pieces of the solution. Studies show that wary individuals have a 42% higher bet of early destruction than extra confident people. Regardless, both laughing and a helpful point of view on life can decrease pressure, perhaps hauling out your life. to our telomeres. Be more dependable

Unwavering quality insinuates a singular's ability to be self-prepared, facilitated, powerful, and objective arranged. Considering data from a survey that followed 1,500 young fellows and young women into old age, kids who were seen as indefatigable, composed and controlled lived 11% longer than their less dependable accomplices. Dedicated people may in like manner have a lower heartbeat and fewer mental conditions, as well as a lower opportunity of diabetes and heart or joint issues. This might be generally considering the way that principled individuals are less disposed to confront risky difficulties or answer unfavorably to strain and bound to continue with productive master presences or be careful about their prosperity.

Qualms can be made at any stage in life through steps as little as tidying up a workspace, sticking to a work plan, or being on time.

15. Drink coffee or tea

Both coffee and tea are associated with a lessened bet of constant infection. For instance, the polyphenols and catechins found in green tea could reduce your bet of threatening development, diabetes, and coronary sickness.

Basically, coffee is associated with a lower opportunity of type 2 diabetes, coronary sickness, and certain illnesses and brain sicknesses, similar to Alzheimer's and Parkinson's. Besides, both coffee and tea purchasers benefit from a 20-30% lower peril of early destruction appeared differently concerning non-buyers. Just review that an overabundance of caffeine can similarly incite apprehension and a dozing issue, so you could have to control your admission to the recommended farthest reaches of 400 mg every day — around 4 cups of coffee. It's moreover critical that it overall requires six hours for caffeine's possessions to subside. Thus, expecting you to experience trouble getting adequate extraordinary rest, you could have to move your admission to earlier in the day.

CULTIVATE A FAIR RESTING PATTERN

Rest is crucial for coordinating cell capacity and helping your body with patching. Another report reports that life expectancy is sensible associated with common resting plans, for instance, going to rest and arousing around a comparative time consistently. Rest term in like manner is apparently a component, with both unnecessarily little and a great deal being destructive.

For instance, resting under 5-7 hours out of each night is associated with a 12% more serious bet of early passing, while simultaneously napping beyond what 8-9 hours of the night could similarly reduce your future by up to 38%. Too little reprieve may similarly propel exacerbation and augmentation of your bet of diabetes, coronary disease, and bulkiness. These are certainly associated with a condensed future. On the other hand, irrational rest could be associated with horror, low dynamic work, and unseen illnesses, all of which may unfavorably impact your future.

DRINK COFFEE OR TEA

B oth coffee and tea are associated with a lessened bet of constant infection. For instance, the polyphenols and catechins found in green tea could reduce your bet of threatening development, diabetes, and coronary sickness.

Basically, coffee is associated with a lower opportunity of type 2 diabetes, coronary sickness, and certain illnesses and brain sicknesses, similar to Alzheimer's and Parkinson's. Besides, both coffee and tea purchasers benefit from a 20-30% lower peril of early destruction appeared differently concerning non-buyers. Just review that an overabundance of caffeine can similarly incite apprehension and a dozing issue, so you could have to control your admission to the recommended farthest reaches of 400 mg every day — around 4 cups of coffee. It's moreover critical that it overall requires six hours for caffeine's possessions to subside. Thus, expecting you to experience trouble getting adequate extraordinary rest, you could have to move your admission to earlier in the day.

CONCLUSION

Life length could give off an impression of being beyond your span, but various strong penchants could lead you to a prepared, old age. These integrate drinking coffee or tea, working out, eating a plant-base diet, getting adequate rest, confining your alcohol confirmation, and more Taken together, these inclinations can uphold your prosperity and put you heading to a long life

www.ingramcontent.com/pod-product-compliance
Lightning Source LLC
Chambersburg PA
CBHW070224180726
47999CB00017B/2304